# Blue
## the Black Fish

The Evolution of a Navy SEAL

## STEVEN KING

iUniverse, Inc.
New York   Bloomington

Blue the Black Fish
The Evolution of a Navy SEAL
VISIT www.bluetheblackfish.com
Cover photos courtesy of Vannita Springer

iUniverse books may be ordered through booksellers or by contacting:

iUniverse
1663 Liberty Drive
Bloomington, IN 47403
www.iuniverse.com
1-800-Authors (1-800-288-4677)

Because of the dynamic nature of the Internet, any Web addresses or
links contained in this book may have changed since publication and
may no longer be valid. The views expressed in this work are solely those
of the author and do not necessarily reflect the views of the publisher,
and the publisher hereby disclaims any responsibility for them.

ISBN: 978-1-4502-0831-4 (pbk)
ISBN: 978-1-4502-0830-7 (ebk)

Printed in the United States of America

iUniverse rev. date: 3/3/2010

This book is dedicated to the
Navy SEALs
Past, Present and Future

**Navy SEAL** - a member of an elite Naval Special Warfare unit who is trained for unconventional warfare; "**SEAL** is an acronym for Sea Air and Land"

*\*Note from the Author:* This book is the culmination of five years of in depth interviews and research into the evolution of a Navy SEAL. It explores the transformation of a young boy whose intense interest in swimming and desire to be the best, led to his induction into one of the world's most elite fighting forces.

You are invited to explore authentic, day-to-day experiences as documented in his 1975 journal of Basic Underwater Demolition SEAL training.

While the technique of BUD/S has evolved over the years, the culture of over achievement remains the same. SEAL instructors will forever echo the motto: "It Pays To Be A Winner"

It was another hot and humid Saturday at the city pool. The sun was high and wispy white clouds streaked across the light blue sky in interesting patterns that slowly morphed into a series of irregular shapes. An occasional hot breeze stirred the still, sticky air as the temperature hovered in the high 90s.

The pool was crowded with children of all ages; some swimming, some floating leisurely under the intense summer sun, while others just splashed about in the shallow end creating undulating waves as they played in the pool's clear blue water. A rambunctious child filled with youthful energy and unchained bravado, was showing off. Egged on by several other boys, he deftly jumped in the pool feet first with his arms extending upward. Instantaneously, any semblance of skill vanished as things went from fun in the sun, to the sheer panic of drowning.

The frantic mother's scream pierced the jovial sounds of laughter as the ever-vigilant lifeguard jolted into action. He spotted the floundering child and blew his whistle making a shrill sound that immediately focused the attention of swimmers and bystanders alike. People were scrambling to get on the pool deck as the lifeguard instinctively dove from his perch into the chilly water. He quickly negotiated between and around the scattering bathers and swam to the youngster in record time, although it seemed like an eternity to the child's mother whose body was as tense as a taut guitar string and her heart was pounding like a drum. Swiftly and with relative ease, the lifeguard brought the child out of the water and gently laid him down at poolside. The boy's small body was limp and a quick check of the child's pulse indicated a heart beat but more than a few seconds had passed and there was no indication that the child was breathing. There was an eerie quiet as people looked on with both anticipation and dread. The lifeguard tilted the child's head back to clear his airway. As he pinched the nose and leaned close to execute rescue breathing, the boy spontaneously sputtered small spurts of water and simultaneously emitted noises that were a combination of coughing, gagging and crying.

A horrified mother, now crouching by her son's side, heaved an audible sigh of relief. Her son seemed to be out of danger. The lifeguard smiled and reassured her that everything was ok. The tension that had enveloped the crowd quickly dissipated as the pool began to fill with children who, because of the frightening incident, were now playing in the water with a bit more caution than usual.

The lifeguard was very relieved that a potentially deadly crisis had been averted. He was also feeling a sense of pride that he had skillfully executed his duties by successfully rescuing the young bather. He returned to his stand and like an eagle with long outstretched wings resumed his watch over the community pool. This alert, attentive lifeguard is an eighteen year-old high school senior.

All stories worth telling have a beginning. This story begins in 1955 in the central Florida town of Orlando where Theodis Springer was born.

At the age of five he moved to the small Atlantic coast town of Stuart, Florida. Theodis, who preferred to be called Theo, was one of six children who lived with their mother, on the east side of Stuart throughout the 1960's. Friends and family called Theo "Blue" and that nickname would follow him for the rest of his life.

Theo was like most black kids growing up in Stuart; he went to school and played hard. However, he was different from most black kids because of his fascination with the water and his desire to excel as a swimmer. Whenever possible, he would watch Seahunt, a very popular underwater action television series that featured a former Navy Frogman turned undersea investigator. In Seahunt the star Mike Nelson became a free agent and operated from his boat the *Argonaut*. In the true spirit of a Navy Frogman Nelson performed salvage operations, rescues and got involved in anything that might happen in the water. Hundreds if not thousands of people were inspired to become divers as Seahunt introduced many, including a young Theo Springer to a whole new undersea world.

Growing up Theo would visit the beach a few times a year and there was no pool to speak of in his community. He went to the Eagle Army Navy store in Stuart and bought his first kiddy fins and kiddy diving mask. His mother would not splurge for such non-essential items so Theo hustled to buy his swim gear. Theo cut grass in the neighborhood and redeemed bottles to pay for the equipment.

The people in the local Eagle Army and Navy store knew him by name. He was the only black kid who would come in and purchase swim items like kiddy diving mask, fins, and face goggles. Even the kids in the neighborhood thought he was crazy. Some would point fingers and laugh; other would make comments like, "Man you can't swim with that stuff" or "boy! You're crazy". He didn't care because he knew with every aspect of his being that he would become a great swimmer.

Outside of the occasional visit to the beach Theodis did not have a place to even try to learn to swim.
During his beach visits, he did little more than wear his fins and goggles as he waded along the shore pretending to be the star in Seahunt.

This all changed one day when Theodis was about twelve years old. One of his friends took him to the mud hole. The mud hole was a retention pond for the city's water treatment plant. It was about the size of an average hotel pool and twelve feet deep in places. The water was milky white and surrounded by mounds of crushed limestone. Determined to learn how to swim he bought several books on swimming. Theo was able to dog paddle around the mud hole with difficulty and. he would practice swim moves on the ground and on his bedroom floor as he set out to learn how to propel himself through the water. The mud hole was off limits and Theo and his friends had to keep their clandestine activities at this retention pond from parents. They developed a code to communicate when they would meet. Hum-guava was the code name.

The mud hole was located about half a mile from his neighborhood .It was murky and unclean but it was the only place that Theo had to practice what he read in his swimming books. Theo would visit almost daily in the summer and on weekends during the school year. Theo and his friends would put Vaseline on their skin after swimming in the mud hole. This hid their limestone-chapped skin from parents.

Theo was popular in high school and had a diverse group of friends. At the age of fifteen he noticed that after school some of his friends would get on a school bus and drive off to an event of some kind. Theo asked one of his buddies boarding the bus where he was going. The young man replied that he was a member of the school swim team and he was off to practice.

Theo watched them drive off and knew that he wanted to be on that bus. Theo ran as fast as he could home, all the while thinking how he would love to be a member of the team. He bought a gym bag and some baggy swim trunks that very afternoon.

The following day, the swim team bus pulled up with the coach at the wheel. Theodis Springer climbed aboard, along with the team, and sat down. Theo asked the coach if he could join the swim team and Coach Dick Wells said, "sure son lets go". They drove the twenty or so miles from Stuart to Ft. Pierce Indian River Community College pool.

Theodis looked out at the Olympic sized swimming pool and stood in awe at the clear blue water. There were diving boards and the racing lanes were clearly marked. This state of the art pool facility was a far cry from the mud hole where Blue and his friends swam in Stuart. Coach Wells told Theo that if he were going to be a member of the swim team he would need the proper swim attire. Wells handed Theo his very first pair of black Speedo swim trunks.
Blue hit the locker room and changed into the Speedo trunks. He returned to the pool edge and prepared to enter the water.

On that day 15 year old high school sophomore Theodis Springer entered an actual swimming pool for the first time in his life.

Coach Wells immediately noticed Theo's rudimentary swimming style and took special interest in helping him develop swimming skills. Under the tutelage of Coach Wells, Theo spent the next couple of months practicing the fundamentals of swimming. Much of this time was spent doing nothing but learning how to properly kick his feet behind a kick board.

The outside most lane of the pool became known as Blue's lane as this is where Theo spent countless hours focusing on swimming basics. The rest of the team honed their swimming skills racing the clock and each other in search of better performance.

Blue learned quickly and progressed to master the freestyle and breaststroke.
By the end of his sophomore year Theodis Springer was competing. Coach Wells and the team all rallied around Blue, encouraging him during every meet. Theo's challenges were far greater than just that of swimming; he also had to overcome the challenges of racial bigotry.

One day the team traveled south to Lake Worth to compete, everyone exited the bus and entered the locker rooms. Theo and a teammate took their time getting off the school bus and walked into the building.

The boys were stopped and told that Theo could not pass through. Blue tried to convince the guy he was part of the team while his teammate ran for help. Coach Wells immediately returned and confirmed that Blue was a swim team member. Although Theo lost his heat, he gained a life long friendship with some of his teammates as well as his coach. It was Coach Wells, who encouraged Theo to lifeguard over the summers.

Blue's swim team involvement fueled his passion for water activities. He became a Red Cross water safety instructor and was certified to teach lifeguarding and swimming.

Theo spent his high school sophomore and junior summer vacations teaching others to swim. One of his classes was featured in the local newspaper. Blue was confident in the water at this point and was signing his name on informal notes…Blue the Black Fish.

In 1974, Blue was a senior in high school. He aspired to go to college. Theo wanted to teach history and coach swimming. He was contemplating a stint in the military as a way to pay for his college education.

Blue received pamphlets from all armed service branches. One particular brochure stood out to Theodis. The brochure showed a group stealthily coming out of the water. It showed guys repelling from helicopters, on jungle patrol and performing underwater demolitions work. This specialized group also retrieved the space capsule and astronauts from the ocean after splash down. The brochure said, "Be Someone Special, Be a Navy SEAL". Theo was enthralled with the advertisement and decided at that moment he was going to join the Navy and become a SEAL.

In June of 1974 on the morning of his senior graduation, Theo went to the Navy recruiter in Ft. Pierce and began the enlistment process. With pamphlet in hand, Theo sat across from the recruiter and explained his desire to become a SEAL. The recruiter chuckled as he stared back at the black recruit, and then instructed him to fill out the forms. Two months later Blue was shipped off to Orlando to begin Navy boot camp.

The first day of Navy boot camp began Theo's four-year enlistment. Day one was described as chaos. Moving from a free spirited high school experience to the structure of Armed forces basic training was taxing to Blue. At the time Navy boot camp was very demanding but Theo described the overall experience as a cakewalk compared to some of the future trials and tribulations he would encounter.

During the first week of training you have to take a swim test. You must be able to swim or to agree to let the Navy teach you how to swim. Theo's unit marched down to the pool in order for their swimming skills to be assessed. Blue was so excited as he jumped in and swam. He quickly demonstrated that he met all the Navy swim requirements. Others in Theo's unit were not so lucky. Blue remembers many of his unit could not swim at all.

Part of the swim requirement was to jump in the water off of a diving board. Some members of the unit clung to the diving board like a scared dog or cat and had to be prodded into the water with a pole. Some were jokingly threatened with a court martial in order to get them in the water. The Navy of course had people in the water to assist so no one would drown.

Navy Boot camp had a company called the Rock Company. This consisted of all the recruits that could not swim. Theo recalls that young black sailors made up the majority of the company. Rock Company recruits spent their time learning how to swim before continuing on with their basic training.

Navy boot camp was nine weeks long and on the fifth week they had what was called service week. This is where the recruits got a chance to work in various occupations throughout the base.

Blue thought that with his lifeguard and swimming background he would be able to spend service week assisting at the pool. Instead of a week at the pool, Blue spent service week working in the mess hall.

Blue made it no secret that he wanted to be a Navy SEAL. His boot camp company commander told Theo that he really didn't want to be a SEAL. He said training was rigorous and most men failed. Blue was determined to pursue SEAL training later on down the line. For now Naval boot camp graduation consumed his thoughts. Blue volunteered for many leadership positions in his company but was passed over by his chain of command.

Theo passed boot camp and requested a job as an Oceanographic Specialist. The Navy had other ideas and assigned Blue to an

Amphibious Construction Battalion stationed in Little Creek Virginia. Blue didn't really pay attention to where he was assigned. His recruit class was sent to assignments all across the globe and Blue's luck of the draw just happened to be the Little Creek Naval Amphibious base in Norfolk Virginia.

Blue arrived at Little Creek with several other recruits. Although he was assigned to the Amphibious Construction Battalion he did not have a specific job rating. He was presented with the option of being a Yeoman. The primary job of the Construction Battalion was constructing pontoon bridges. The Yeoman slot was an administration position that was an office job. Theo preferred the inside work to the cold windy waterfront where the construction occurred. Blue had taken a high school typing course that came in handy with his new job.

Blue soon discovered that Little Creek housed various amphibious units and most importantly is the east coast home base for the United States Navy SEALs.

Theo began training whenever possible for the strenuous Navy SEAL assessment test. He told his immediate supervisor of his desire to be a SEAL. The supervisor said "Blue don't be glory hunting, you don't want to be a Navy Frogman just do your job here and be a good clerk".

Another name for Navy SEALs is Navy Frogmen. Before the SEALs were commissioned in 1962 the World War II underwater demolition teams were called Frogmen. Blue most certainly did want to be a Frogman. The fact that Theo's barracks was across the street from where Navy SEAL team UDT 21 resided only fueled the drive to pursue his dream. Blue felt that fate brought him to Little Creek for a reason. That reason was crystal clear to the young man from South Florida, he was destined to become be a Navy SEAL.

On weekends when his buddies were going to clubs Blue was exercising in his room preparing himself to apply for SEAL training. Theo spent the next few months working in administration and working out.

Theo was jogging along the beach one evening and found a partial page from a demolition instruction manual. Theo ran along the same beach where the Navy SEALs trained. Theo would hear the explosions from the base and get even more excited about becoming a Navy SEAL.

During one of Blue's evening beach runs he encountered a Navy SEAL from UDT 21. Theo jogged alongside the sailor and told him of his wish join a SEAL team. The SEAL gave Theo a pair of jungle boots and told him to run in them. The two became friends and Theo was able to get a few hints on how to prepare for SEAL training.

In March of 1975 Theo met with the recruiter for the east coast SEAL teams and provided the necessary paperwork. The recruiter put Blue through the initial physical assessment, which consisted of pushups, sit-ups, running and swimming. Blue fulfilled all the physical requirements and his completed application was submitted to the Bureau of Naval Personal. In Theo's mind he was on the way to training and would soon be shipped to San Diego California for Basic Underwater Demolition SEAL training commonly known as BUD/S.

Six weeks passed before Theo received a letter from the Navy.

Theo opened the letter and was saddened to see that he had been denied entrance to BUD/S. According to the letter his ASVAB score was five points below the requirement. The Armed Forces Vocational Aptitude Battery was designed to measure an individual's aptitude to be trained in a specific job.

Theo was resolved to become a Navy Frogman and was determined to raise his score and retake the SEAL assessment. Blue was told that he could reapply in six months to become a Navy SEAL trainee.

Theo did not have to wait six months; two months later the SEAL recruiter called and said that they had lowered the score requirement on the written test. Blue was encouraged to reapply immediately.

Theo was an administration guy so the next day he resubmitted his request for SEAL training to the Navy for consideration. Theo was optimistic this time and Blue began telling his friends that he was going to California for SEAL training.

A few weeks later another letter from the Navy arrived. This time the letter said that he had been accepted for Navy SEAL training.

Theo went back to work and typed up his own orders and submitted them for the appropriate signatures.

Theo flew to San Diego, California and then drove to the Coronado Naval Amphibious Base to begin training. The SEAL trainees were housed in a special barracks on base. The trainees were given about two weeks to acclimate themselves to the California weather. This first couple of weeks was not very regimented. The trainees were not an actual class yet and had a lot of free time. They spent their days working out and running along the beach in an attempt to get in condition.

Blue's training barracks was fifty feet from the ocean and adjacent to where the three west coast SEAL teams were housed. SEAL Team 1 was in the next building. Blue would see the team guys doing their thing wearing the coveted blue and gold reserved for actual SEAL team members.

Trainees were issued green t-shirts and khaki UDT swim trunks during the training phase. BUD/S' training is twenty-three weeks long and broken into three primary phases. The trainees wore one of three different colored helmets to designate what phase of training they were in. Green helmets signified the first phase, which consisted of physical conditioning and classroom work. Phase two trainees wore red helmets. The red helmet phase was where the trainees learned land warfare and demolition. The third and final phase trainees wore blue helmets to show that they were learning scuba diving and underwater operations.

If all went according to plan Blue would finish the course as a Navy SEAL. Twenty-three weeks is a long time and a lot could go wrong for Theo. Blue talked to quite a few people who had attempted SEAL training only to fail. Theo saw the various green, red and blue helmeted classes conducting training at the base. Blue knew that his time had come to see if he could hack the intense physical and mental conditioning required to be a SEAL.

The SEAL literature that Blue read clearly stated that a Navy SEALs performance should be ten times greater than that of an average man.

There was a shiny brass bell next to the Navy SEAL instructor's office. The bell was the way for a trainee to ring out of SEAL training. When a trainee had enough, he rang the bell three times to signify quitting. He would be dropped from the program and sent back to the fleet. No questions asked. Blue would hear the bell ring often during those first two weeks. It was a chilling sound to know that every time the bell rang it meant another trainee just couldn't hack it. Theo was excited and nervous about his upcoming training.

In the two weeks of conditioning before day one of training the new trainees were becoming confident. They could run miles along the beach and exercise with ease. Occasionally one of the SEAL team guys would congratulate them on making the cut and welcome them to sunny California. Blue thought that these SEAL guys were nice and very cordial. He began to think that Navy SEAL training couldn't be all that hard. After all, he was in prime shape and ready for anything.

So he thought.

Basic Underwater Demolition SEAL training class 86 was officially formed. Day one of Navy SEAL training began. Approximately seventy trainees were in the class including Blue. That first day's exercise session wore all the new trainees down to the bone. The SEAL instructors were not just barking out orders. Those instructors did every exercise right along with the trainees. The trainees were left in a frazzled heap while the instructors barely broke a sweat.

After the morning work out the trainees were assembled and the senior instructors addressed the group. The first senior instructor told them that most of them were not going to make it. Of the trainees six were black. The instructor quoted" and you brothers down there, by the time I finish this class I will be able to count all of your asses on one finger". The second senior instructor stepped forward and addressed the trainees. He said that his job was to help you "out" of the program. This instructor issued a simple reminder. He said," all you have to do to return to your former life was to ring the bell three times". He went on to say that this was going to be the hardest thing that any of them would ever do in life. He was powerful and intimidating, the model of a Navy SEAL instructor. Blue was soon to learn that he meant every word he said.

The instructors for class 86 were Navy SEALs fresh from combat tours in Vietnam. The unconventional warfare of the Vietnam conflict is where Navy SEAL teams gained worldwide recognition. The SEAL Team nickname in Vietnam was "Devils with green faces".

Navy SEAL training is a rigorous 23-week course designed to push the limits of ones physical and mental boundaries. Each individual training segment is called an " Evolution" The trainees are referred to as tadpoles. The successful recruit will evolve into a Navy Frogman like a tadpole develops into a frog.

Every Friday afternoon the trainees were given the following weeks training evolutions. They knew exactly what to expect and when to expect it. The structure of BUD/S training is different from most military programs in that you are not quarantined with your peers during the training. Many times you have nights and weekends off.
Some trainees brought their families with them to BUD/S and unless they were conducting an evolution they had free time to spend how they saw fit. Some of the guys would go to clubs until

late at night. They found out the hard way that SEAL instructors did not go easy on the hung over recruit during the next morning's evolution. Blue remembers an instructor's baritone voice telling the class "People if you hoot with the owls all night be prepared to soar with the eagles in the morning". Physical Training is referred to as PT in the military and many of the evolutions have PT as a central theme. Blue spent his free time resting and writing letters home.

Even during your free time during BUD/S it was generally not a good idea to bump into a Navy SEAL instructor. Chances are you would find yourself being interrogated about what you were doing and where you were going. These chance encounters between instructors and trainees usually resulted in some additional PT for the unlucky recruit.

There was no walking allowed during BUD/S. Trainees had to run everywhere for the duration of the training. If an instructor caught a recruit walking a round of at least fifty push-ups was almost guaranteed. SEAL instructors were notorious for making the trainees "drop" and do push-ups. A Navy SEAL push-up is called a four-count push-up. You only count every other push-up. Fifty SEAL push-ups translate to one hundred push-ups in real time.

SEAL instructors carried whistles that were used for training. One whistle blow meant for the trainees to immediately fall to the ground on their stomachs and freeze. Two whistle blows signaled the trainee to begin low crawling along the ground toward the sound of the whistle. Three whistle blows and the trainee was to recover and resume what they had been doing prior to the whistle drill.

Instructors constantly reminded the trainees to pay attention to detail and listen closely when being given instructions. Every infraction discovered by an instructor resulted in some form of disciplinary action. Navy SEAL instructors are known for being ultra creative in how they doled out punishment. Each instructor had his own personality and his own favorite way to deal with the recruits. Some instructors preferred to have the recruits "Get Wet" while others liked to employ physical training as the way to get a particular point across to a wayward trainee.

Being told to "Get Wet" was a way to discipline those that fell short of the mark. Getting wet meant you had to sprint from your location into the Pacific Ocean and return dripping wet with sea water. The recruits would sometimes go wet themselves in the shower instead of going to the sea as instructed. After all it was much more comfortable to get wet in a warm shower instead of the brutally chilly ocean.
To prevent this most of the instructors would tell the recruits to "Get Wet" and be sure and bring back a bottom sample from the Bay. The dark muddy sand was proof that the trainee indeed got wet.

If an instructor felt a trainee was not doing his best during

PT a Goon Squad session was arranged. The Goon Squad was additional PT after the day's evolutions were over. Every week there was a four mile timed run and a timed obstacle course. You were expected to improve your times on a weekly basis or face punishment and the relentless PT of the goon squad.

While the physical requirements placed on a SEAL trainee were extreme to say the least. The mental stress placed on recruits was just as taxing. Along with the physical evolutions the Navy SEAL trainees had to attend evolutions in the classroom. They were expected to be competent in courses like map-making cartography, hydrographic reconnaissance, venomous animals of the sea, combat medicine and diving physics.

On Average 70% to 80% of BUD/S recruits choose to DOR or Drop-On-Request. BUD/S' training is voluntary; hence recruits may opt out at any time. Once a trainee quits he is immediately removed from the training environment and referred to administration for the exit process.

The trainees arrived at various times. The recruits were arriving from US naval posts from around the world. Depending on how fast orders were processed and travel arrangements made determined when the recruit arrived in San Diego. The weeks before the class officially forms are known as pre-training.

Blue stood waist deep in the chilly water of the Pacific Ocean. His core temperature was plummeting. The incessant waves were pounding down on his shivering body. Blue and the rest of Navy SEAL recruit class 86 was standing in what is commonly referred to as the "Surf Zone".

Theo and six other recruits struggled to hold a telephone pole log above their heads. A Navy SEAL instructor paced the sand in front of the men with his deep voice bellowing, " Its mind over matter people, if you don't mind it don't matter". Blue's teeth were chattering as the instructor asked the group if they were cold. The answer to that question was obvious as the recruits fought to stand against the icy waves. The Navy SEAL instructor's piercing eyes looked right through the recruit class as he stated sarcastically " You think you are cold now, people you don't know what cold is". The rumbling voice continued to motivate the recruits to endure by saying" The only easy day was yesterday. You are striving to become a member of a Navy SEAL team. Pull together right here and right now because failure is not an option".

The team of recruits holding the log next to Blue fell forward into the surf. One by one the seven men rose from the water and took hold of their log. Just as they began lifting the log one of the men detached from the group. He stumbled forward and collapsed on the beach in front of the instructor. With a wavering voice and tear filled eyes the recruit looked up at the instructor and announced his decision to quit. The instructor told the recruit to ignore the pain and the cold and fall back in with his squad. This recruit was unable to comply and SEAL training claimed another victim. He slowly rose from the sand and took one last look at the formation of grizzled recruits. He knew that his leaving was going to leave his squad to absorb the weight of the waterlogged telephone pole without him. Guilt consumed him as he searched for internal reserves that were absent. With his mind, body and spirit broken the trainee stumbled to the main compound where he rang the big brass bell outside of the instructor's office three times. This ringing out signified that he no longer had what it took to continue SEAL training. The instructor's eyes scanned the cold wet recruits as he growled "Anybody else want to quit? Navy SEALs don't ever quit. Remember people if you want to wear the name you have to play the game. You don't have to like it, you just have to do it". The recruits were tired and hurting but stood ready for his next command.

The instructor ordered the recruits to keep the log up above their heads and to stand still. A resounding Hoo-Yah from the group ensured that the directive was understood. While Theo's team of recruits faltered they did not fail in their task to keep the log aloft. Blue was learning a valuable lesson in teamwork as the men struggled to do together what none of them could have accomplished alone. Blue was experiencing log physical training, one of the many training "Evolutions" that must be endured to become a United States Navy SEAL.

*Theo kept a daily journal during BUD/S. Let's begin our look into Basic Underwater Demolition SEAL training through the eyes of Blue the Black Fish.*

# The Journey of Tadpole

## Seaman Theodis Springer

4 Sep 75

Today was my first day to check in at BUD/S. I was treated very nice; I didn't expect to be treated so well. The BUD/S compound is separated from the rest of the Amphibious Base. Our barracks is located right on the Pacific Ocean. I can see mountains and everything. California is a beautiful place. There are quite a few black guys in my class. I think that the instructors have a negative attitude about all of us making it. I'm going to do my best to help all of them with their swimming. The instructors seemed to be impressed with the time I got on my swim. I went swimming in the ocean this afternoon. The water was very cold. Tonight five other guys and I went to downtown San Diego. We first checked things out. You can't even buy a beer if you are younger than twenty-one. That SUCKS!! I'm asking God to be with me all the way through BUD/S.

5 Sep 75

Today was my first day to have PT, and it was tough. I've got a long way to go. I ran to break in my boots and we went swimming down to the base pool. Everyone was under the impression that I was an Officer today. I'm starting to eat a good balanced meal now. The food here is a lot better than Little Creek. My body is very sore, so I just stayed in tonight. Here at BUD/S, you have to run everywhere you go. No walking is allowed. Everyone on base knows we are BUD/S trainees because we are always running as a group or even when we are alone. I'm going to see Chicago and War next Sunday. I'm willing to pay any price to see them.

6/7 Sep 75

Saturday I went down town to buy tickets to the Chicago and War concert. We also ran the beach. Today I just rested up all day. I was talking and drinking with some of the guys in Class 84 last night. And, from what they tell me this training will be very very tough. I think I'm going to have a problem with the weather. Right now it even feels like winter to me. I'm just asking God to be with me and help me make it through these next six months.

8 Sep 75

Today we started pre training. We did PT on the beach then we saw a movie. Tomorrow we will swim in the pool. We also had to do our clean up detail. I've been thinking a lot about a girl from home. I have a few of her pictures up in my locker. I've been feeling very bored.

There's not too much to do right now, but when training starts, Ill be very busy. I went running this afternoon after evening chow. I'd like to get real tight with someone.

9 Sep 75

Today we went to the pool and swam. I was picked as an instructor. We swam races and I got very exhausted. I went to the Naval Air Station to look for some brasso brass cleaner. We are going to have a Big Inspection tomorrow.

10/11 Sep 75

We did about the same thing for the past few days. We ran a few miles and we swam relays in the pool. I was picked as one of the class instructors. I've been helping a buddy with his swimming.

I also was picked as a team Captain of one of the relay teams. We won yesterday and almost today I did all right in the running yesterday too. Tomorrow we will be timed in the 300-yard swim and the mile run. I am not going to swim the 300-yard swim fast because I think that if I did, the instructors will be expecting me to do well all the time.

We got a new Black guy in today. He's from San Diego. He said he swam the 300 in 5:15, two second better than me. He also says he has his WSI (Water Safety instructor). He'll be about the second black that I've met with a WSI certification. I'd like to see all of us make it.

12/13 Sep 75

Friday morning we ran the mile. I came in first place with a 5:58, but I didn't push it that hard. I think I'll do it a lot better the next time. We didn't swim the three hundred yards; maybe we will swim it on Monday. I went to see Deep Throat last night. The movie was not very professional at all. It was very nasty and it had no meaning. We also tried to pick up these two girls but no luck. Today we went to Black's beach but no one was there. Black's beach is a nude beach. I'd never been to a nude beach before. We watched guys hang glide in the air off the cliffs. It was the first time seeing that in person. We just rode all over the place trying to pick up girls. I don't enjoy leading this type of life at all. I've decided to save my money and in about six months; I'm going to buy a car. I plan on having at least $1,000 for a down payment. I went over to the Base Club tonight to have a beer. It's a pretty nice place.

## 14 Sep 75

This morning, we got up early to go to the concert. My buddy is a Mexican guy who is from Brownsville, TX. We workout together and are good friends. We are both E-3s. The concert was at the San Diego baseball stadium. There was a very large crowd. I was so excited. The group Poco was on first. War performed second and they were fantastic. Chicago was third and they were Great!! I was up front when they came on. They were just as great as I expected them to be. They did all the songs we did back in band. I knew all the songs. After the concert, I bought a Chicago poster. I had never been to a big stadium like that before. There were a lot of good-looking young ladies there. A lot of Hippies were there too. People were drinking wine and smoking Pot all over the place right in front of the police. Tomorrow is payday. I thank God for letting one of my dreams come true.

15 Sep 75

Today was payday, so that started the day off all right. I got paid my Leave rations. That helped out a lot. I couldn't even find a sweat suit that I liked. I went over to the base store to shop. My team came in first place today. We are to get a new Black guy in the class tomorrow. I hope He's good in swimming. I just hope that God stays with him and helps him make it. We went over to the Enlisted Men (EM) Club and had a beer then went to a pizza place for a pizza. I wrote Mother tonight and sent her $100.

16 Sep 75

Today wasn't too hard of a day. We didn't have to go to the pool. We spent time in the classroom. We are going to have a beer party on Friday. We all put in $2 towards the party. I bought a new lock for my locker and a new alarm clock. I think that "Sugar Bear" the new black dude is a little weird. I'm still trying to figure what type of guy he is. I don't think that we'll get real tight. I went running tonight with a guy, it was a pretty good run. After the run, we ordered a pizza. I can't wait to get some mail. I think I'm going to send $100 to my savings account. Today was a nice sunny day.

19 Sep 75

For the past few days' things have been going ok. We have one more week of pre Training. We've been swimming in the ocean for the past few days. We had a party this afternoon and it was all right. A few guys went streaking down the beach. I think that we may get into a little trouble about it on Monday. I wrote a letter home the other day. I sent $100 home to my bank. My buddy likes white girls a lot. So we do have something in common… We went to the club tonight and we were rapping with these two white girls. I thought they were too young. I could tell that he was enjoying it all. I think that he was raised in a middle class type family.

He has a lot of weird ways about himself. I think he tries to portray the Soul brother image to me. But I think that he is all right. He's into that KUNG FU crap, which I don't care for, and he's always jiving around and I don't like it. But, he's a pretty cool dude.


20/21 Sep 75

Saturday I went camping out in the mountains with three other guys in my class. We climbed to the top of the mountain it was very beautiful view from the top. This was my very first time ever being in the mountains. We slept out there over night. Today on the way back up one side of a cliff, I almost got stuck up the side with no way out. I finally made it out. It was really scary. We went back to Black's Beach this afternoon. There were actually some beautiful girls there, all in the nude. I really felt embarrassed and didn't take off my clothes. People were playing volleyball and other games on the beach in the nude.


22 Sept 75

Today was all right but I did poor on my 300-yard swim. I got fourth place. I didn't expect to do that bad. I got the pictures of

Chicago today and they came out all right. Pre training is getting harder. I am terrified about what we will have to endure once real training starts. I'm going to put out all I have. I'm asking God to be with me.


23 Sept 75

Today we did our PT with instructor T instead of Chief R. He seems to be an all right guy but I don't like him as much as Chief R. We swam the 300 yards again today. I got fourth place. I went to down town San Diego tonight. I called mother tonight, she seemed very happy about the money I sent. She said that my old girl friend asked about me. That makes me feel pretty good.


24 Sept 75

I missed the PT this morning; I went to dental to make an appointment. I'll be going back Friday to get some work done. The new Black dude checked in today. They say that he can swim and that he's done some competitive swimming but he's worried about his running. I got very sick today in the chow hall. After I rested a while, I felt better. This afternoon I went to the pool and helped a buddy and met his wife. She's a nice girl.

He seems to be very happy with her and that's good. I ran a little tonight then I came in and showered up before writing a letter.


25 Sept 75

We ran pretty well today in PT. Then we swam the 300 yards. I still got fourth place. I'd like to get a lot better. I got a letter from a buddy today; he seems to be doing fine back at Little Creek.

He is a white guy from Mass. We had lots of fun together while serving at the Amphibious Construction Battalion Two.

26 Sept 75
Today I missed PT. I went to the dentist and had my front tooth fixed along with my back teeth in order to improve my bite. There are six of us brothers in the class now; two new ones came in today. Tonight at the club I met this beautiful black chick from Rhode Island. She was so beautiful and sounded so sweet. I wish she wasn't married, but says she's happily married. I met a new guy in our class tonight. A guy in class 85 is getting to be a good friend of mine.

27 Sept 75
Today I went to LA and Hollywood. It was all right but sort of a disappointment. There were a lot of Hispanic people there. I can't speak Spanish so I just looked around. There were a lot of beautiful women there. We went to the Hollywood Wax Museum. It wasn't as good as I thought it would be. We just jived around and then came home. We stopped in Long Beach and visited Pike's Peak. It was fun. I won a few prizes. I received a letter from mother today and a bank statement. She sent me my swimsuit. Tomorrow I have to cut off all of my hair... I ran out of money tonight so a buddy paid for most of the trip.

28 Sept 75
Today we cleaned up rooms and got everything squared way. I shaved my head and I Love it!! Everyone got haircuts. There are a

lot of new recruits in today and I'd like to see all of make it. But, I know only a few will. I'm asking God to help us all. A friend paid for my food tonight because I went to Burger King.

29 Sept 75

Today was all right but the Obstacle Course was very tough. It made me very tired. We spent about three hours on PT. We almost missed chow. Tomorrow we are going to spend a lot of time at the pool. Tomorrow's also Pay Day!!!!

30 Sept 75

We had an inspection this morning and I did all right. But I need to improve. We just ran a mile then we went over to the pool and swam the 300-yard swim. I swam it in 5:18.

I'm still in the upper part of the class, but not the best. I was also chosen to teach today. Then we had relay races. I wish I were together with my swimming. While I'm swimming, I tend to dislike it and I'm not relaxed.

But, I guess I will get better. The instructors haven't been breaking our horns us as much as I had expected. I don't seem to understand why they are so nice to us… Payday was today and I'm sending $115.00 home to the bank. I wrote home tonight. A friend didn't pass the swim today. I hope he gets his shit together by next Thursday.

01 Oct 75

We ran the O course today and I did it in 14:40, I just did make the cut off time. I just can't do that damn obstacle called "DIRTY

NAME". Each time I attempt to jump up to the higher log, it just kills me. We were indoctrinated on the IBS (Inflatable Boat Small) today .I think that they are going to be a lot of fun. One of the new Brothers seems to be a pretty cool dude.

02 Oct 75

Today we swam most of the day. It wasn't really that hard, but I took it as kind of tough.

Tonight I went out to dinner at Captain Jake's. I blew $10 on nothing. That pissed me off. We talked to some black dudes in the SEAL Teams. They were giving us a few words of wisdom.

3-4 Oct 75

Friday we finished up another week. We ran the O course and I brought my time down to 12:28. We ran, then after lunch we had PT until we secured at about 1430 hours. I went to see the movie The God Father II. It wasn't that good. Today I went to the pool to swim. An instructor was there and he wasn't very friendly. I think he's on some kind of ego trip. Tonight I went to a pizza place to eat. I have a lot of things to do to prepare for the inspection on Monday.

7 Oct 75

Today we did a 3½ mile run and IBS Surf Passage. I love the surf passage but I hate the cold water. I got so cold today. I just don't know what I'm going to do come Hell Week. After lunch, we swam a while in the pool. The instructors are making us do all kinds of fucked –up shit. They just love to see us suffer. My roommate is having problems with his running. I think he hurt his leg the other day. I have my doubts about him making it through this class. I'm asking god to help me make it through the class.

8 Oct 75

We had IBS surf passage again today. It still was a lot of fun even though it was cold. But, I'm going to hang in there. I lowered my time in the O Course. I think that the instructors like me a little. They are expecting me to do well in the training. Tomorrow is the day of the swim test.

I plan to take first in the Mile run. I don't know if I should try my best in the 300-yard swim or not. I think that we will lose a few guys tomorrow.

9-10 Oct 75

Yesterday was the swim test. A few people failed it. Two of the other black guys rang out. Today we had a four mile timed run. I got 2nd place with a 29:37 time. Then we ran the O Course. I did a 16-minute time. They added the obstacle "SLIDE FOR LIFE" to the O course. Tonight some buddies and I went to San Diego to check it out. We later went to get something to eat at Pizza Galore. On the way home we were stopped by a Cop and searched for Pot. Today was our last day of Pre-Training. Tuesday is the big day. I have got to get my stuff together on the O Course.

11 Oct 75

I slept till 1100 hours today. I then got up and had something to eat. I did laundry today.

12 Oct 75

Today I went riding all over town just checking things out. I mailed a letter home. I hope they return it. At times, I don't seem to like my roommate's attitude. But, I guess I'll never find a person who's the perfect Theodis!

*Tuesday October 14, 1975 was the official first day of the 23-week BUD/S course for class 86. Blue writes:*

14 Oct.

Today was our first day of training. We spray painted our helmets green to show that we were a class in phase one of BUD/S. We had Physical Training at 5:00 in the morning and a very fast four-mile run. I almost died on the obstacle course. My arms were like lead by the time I got to the cargo net. I was the last person in on the obstacle course. I did terrible.

15 Oct.

Today I ran another 4 miles. It wasn't as hard as before. I brought my time down on the obstacle course from 23 minutes to 19:05. I sure am hurting on these evolutions. It hurts so bad that the thought of quitting runs through my mind. I am going to stick it out. I am asking God to be with me.

16 Oct.

Today was a pretty easy day. Only a few people got wet during the barracks inspection. I got wet this morning during PT. The instructor asked me what my problem was and why I wasn't doing a good time on the obstacle course.

All three of my roommates got the goon squad tonight. I hope I never have to get it. But if I don't get my shit together on the obstacle course I will. I am asking God to be with me during this training.

17 Oct.

We finished up the first week of training today. We had a three-mile soft sand run and it was a bitch. One of the recruits fell way back on the run. An instructor was on his case like a bum on a ham sandwich. The instructor jogged next to the fallback yelling at him to catch up. When that did not work the instructor picked the trainee up by the back of his shirt. The recruit was lifted off the ground and it looked like he was running in air. Instructor T. caught up to the rest of the group dangling the recruit in the air with one hand. The instructor dropped the recruit back into our formation. I would have never believed it unless I had seen it with my own two eyes. Man these instructors are tough, like wild animals. We had drown proofing after lunch. They tied my hands behind my back and tied my feet together. I had to hop into the pool and swim 25 yards underwater. This was a survival tactic to ensure that we could survive in the water if tied up. After the pool the instructor made us march into the bay and do handstands in the water. It was kind of fun but the water was very cold. I want to thank God for helping me this far.

20 Oct.

Today in training we had our final drown proofing practical. We had to swim 50 yards underwater. I did it!! I can't believe it. It was real tough but I did it. I thank God.

21 Oct.

Today we had to swim in the cold ass ocean and I mean it was cold! I couldn't believe how much my body was shivering. There were some big waves out there and I almost drowned. My swim buddy and I had a ½ mile swim with fins. I did not do too hot. The instructor busted me for swimming more than 6 feet away from my swim buddy. I brought my obstacle course time down to 13:29. My roommate rang out. I've made it through another day. Thank God.

22 Oct 75

We had a mile Bay swim today and used fins and mask. I had a little difficulty with the fins. Tonight we had stealth and concealment training on the beach. While we were hiding near some rocks, The Senior Chief spit tobacco on us for twenty minutes. He was talking to another instructor about how well we were hiding and that he could not see us, yea right! That was a trip… After he grew tired of his game with us he told us all to get wet and hide better next time because our lives would depend on it. We had to hit the surf. My swim buddy and I were the last two to come in. We got goon squad that night for being last.

*Along with the physical training and swimming evolutions the trainees were learning their semaphore skills. Semaphore is signaling with flags. They also had to master the dots and dashes of Morse code by flashlight. By this time in the training the recruits had been introduced to the famous rubber boats that SEAL teams use on missions. This watercraft is called Inflatable Boat Small or IBS. An IBS holds up to seven people. Six row while the seventh steers. Initial IBS training is called surf passage. The recruits learn how to maneuver the boats into the ocean from the beach. The waves are huge and the team must work together in order to get through the surf. On the way back to shore the boat would attempt to ride the waves in. The team members would always scan the water for large waves. Someone would yell "water" in order to warn the group to brace themselves for an incoming wave. The wave would smash into the small boat scattering the men into the frigid water like so many match sticks. The team would have to regroup in the ocean and try again or face the wrath of an ever-present SEAL instructor. The recruits also had to learn what was called rock portage. This was the extremely dangerous task of landing your IBS on jagged barnacle covered rocks. During IBS training the recruits wore bulky orange life jackets. Blue writes:*

23 Oct 75

We had the IBS and Rock Portage today. It was murder. Everyone was scared to death. I got my hands cut from the barnacles on the rocks. The objective was to land the IBS on the rocks while each member attempts to exit the boat. We paddled out into the ocean, and then we were given the command to land on the rocks. The waves were very rough and would force the IBS against the rocks. The key to rock portage was to paddle in sync and attempt to time the force of the wave.

Once you have made contact with the rocks, the number one man would jump out of the boat grabbing the towline and pull the boat up onto the rocks. All the while you are fighting the force of the incoming waves throwing you against the rocks. It was really a frightening experience. We have rock portage next Wednesday night. We also had a five-½ mile run and it was pretty tough. I don't seem to be enjoying this training. I hate every Evolution. I've got to get my head together. I thank God I'm alive today. A few people got really hurt on the rock portage today.

24-27 Oct 75

We've had a three day weekend and so I've been relaxing and taking it easy. I've been studying my Morse code and Semaphore. I just hung out Saturday and Sunday. I went to check out some vans. I test drove a Chevy van and it was great and completely loaded. The price of the van was $8000 with payments of $200 a month for 36 months. I doubt that I'll be getting that one. I can buy a Vet or a Trans-Am for that price.

Today I cleaned all my gear and the room for tomorrow's inspection. I called home tonight. Everything is about the same. My car is still there and mother is asking for money and so I'm going to help her out. The next fourteen days will probably be the toughest in my life, so I'm asking God to be with me.

**28 Oct 75**

I really did shitty this morning at PT. All the instructors got in my shit. I'd better get my shit together. We did rock portage this morning till lunch. It was a lot better than before. I brought my O'Course time down into the 12s. In an evolution called Sentry Stalking they taught us how to kill tonight. The method of sneaking up behind the enemy and cutting his throat with a Kay bar, stabbing him in the side, twisting it then pulling it out. This is the first time I felt that this training is for real. I've got to get my flashing light skills together by Friday.

**29-30 Oct 75**

Yesterday we had cast and recovery. It was pretty cool, but the water was just a little cold. Cast and recovery is a method of insertion and extraction by speedboat. While the speedboat travels at a high rate of speed, the swimmer rolls off of the IBS that is attached to the speedboat or jumps from the rear of the speedboat. The swimmers are dropped at twenty-five yard intervals. For the recovery, the swimmer treads water while lifting his left arm above his head. As the high-speed boat approaches to recover the swimmer, you kick vigorously with your swim fins in an attempt to elevate yourself out of the water as high as possible. This was very scary initially because the high-speed boat is coming directly toward you. As the boat approaches, a team member is in the IBS with a rubber device called a snare. The swimmer inserts his left arm into the snare down to his elbow. The swimmer then grabs his left wrist with his right hand. While kicking vigorously the team member pulls the swimmer into the boat. That's why frogmen wear their watches on the right wrist instead of the left wrist. A lost issued watch would be an expensive venture.

We also had night rock portage. The surf wasn't big at all, so it wasn't that hard. There were quite a few towns' people down there watching us. The locals know when we have rock portage. They have a party and seem to enjoy seeing us in pain and getting injured. My boat crew has got to get its shit together with paddling. We had a race back to the barracks and we were the last crew. So, we had to pay for our ineptness. My swim buddy quit on the 2-mile ocean swim today. So I got with another swim pair back to the area. This morning we ran down to the golf course just like yesterday. We had just a little PT. The instructors really fucked us today. They had us in the surf all day. It really sucked. I had the urge to ring that fucking bell. There was no liberty for anyone tonight. Today was payday but no one got to cash his checks.

The instructors actually carry a little tea bell around with them so you can ring out even if you are not on the compound.

31 Oct.

We had a fourteen-mile soft sand beach run today. We ran it all the way with no rest. Afterwards I got cramps all over but I made it. A few people rang out during the run. We had an introduction to hell week lecture this afternoon. I failed my flashing light

Morse code test today. My semaphore test is tomorrow. I will be studying. Hell week starts in two days.

1 Nov.

This morning we had a semaphore test. I don't know what my score was but I think I passed it. I took the flashing light test again and passed this time. I bought a bunch of junk food for hell week. I've just been taking it easy.

*It's the 4th week of training and "Hell Week" began. There were no entries in Blue's journal between Sunday November 2nd and Saturday November 8th 1975. Of the six blacks that started training only two were left including Blue. The others were either dropped or rang out. Most SEAL recruit classes lose the majority of their class during hell week. The recruits were extremely nervous about what to expect. They were used to getting a weekly schedule of evolutions so they could prepare both physically and mentally for what was expected.*

*There was no schedule for hell week; all the recruits knew was to be in the barracks by 9:00 PM Sunday evening. The instructor smirked and advised the recruits to get some sleep because they would need it. The SEAL instructor turned off the lights as he exited and the barracks was immersed in darkness. Blue was unable to sleep so he tossed and turned in his bunk trying to imagine what lay in store for him. The quiet in the barracks was eerie as the recruits awaited their fate. This was the calm before the storm and Blue finally dozed off.*

*At the stroke of Midnight all hell broke lose. The instructors barged
into the barracks firing machine guns and lighting explosives. The
noise was deafening and the bright lights from the explosions was
disorienting. An instructor barked orders for the recruits to get dressed
and assemble outside in an impossible 30 seconds. A few moments
later the group mustered in the chilly California darkness. The SEAL
instructor was staring at his watch. He raised his head and his
deep voice resonated" Its hell week people and you are late for my
formation. All of you go get wet". The group sprinted the 1/4 mile
to the ocean and dove into the frigid water. They returned to the
instructor soaked and cold. Each team was told to grab their IBS. The
six to seven man teams were advised to keep the IBS on their head for
the remainder of the week.*

*When not in an active evolution the rubber boat was to be carried on
the recruits' heads. Due to constant attrition from guys ringing out
or being injured the recruit teams were always being adjusted. The
individual squads of men did not like when one of their team rang
out or was dropped from BUD/S. That meant more work for those
left trying to pick up the slack.*

*An instructor yelled" report to the pool for relay races" and the back-
to-back evolutions of hell week had begun. Competition between the
squads was a constant during BUD/S. This competitive environment
was intensified during hell week. As the recruit teams entered the
pool and raced each other a SEAL instructor paced back and forth
announcing, " It pays to be a winner people, it pays to be a winner".
The recruit teams that came in last were punished while the winning
teams were allowed a few moments of precious rest.*

*Blue and his team were huddled together trying to stay warm while they awaited their next race. The men were clinging to each other using what body heat they had to keep the next man warm. An instructor commented that they were using good judgment and teamwork by sticking close to each other. It was pointed out that the use of body heat might save a life one day in combat. Then the instructor said, "Welcome to hell week", before turning a water hose on Blue's group and soaking them to the bone.*

*Blue described the week as unbearable. The recruits were constantly on the move and they were ringing out on a daily basis. The instructors would only allow 5 or 10 minutes of rest a couple times a day. Many times you did not get the chance to rest because of being punished.*

*In order to simulate the stresses of combat, sleep deprivation was the over all theme of hell week. Blue recalls frequent hallucinations. The trainees spent hours on end paddling through the ocean in the IBS. Blue remembers hallucinating that sea monsters were climbing out of the cold dark ocean. The recruits had grown to depend on each other for motivation. If one man fell the others would grab him and drag him through until the evolution was completed. The instructors would constantly declare that each team was only as strong as its weakest link. The instructors also reminded the recruits that they were not going to kill them. They said other classes had been through hell week and survived and destiny would allow some members of class 86 to make it also. Hell week ultimately determines who has the physical and mental ability to endure the remainder of BUD/S. The* purpose of hell week was to show the trainees that they were capable of amazing feats of endurance. It was a true test of mind over matter as the recruits had to learn to ignore the pain, sand, mud and constant discomfort of being cold and wet.

Hell week is 90% mental and 10% physical, as you must ignore your battered body as it screams out for you to quit. Instructors want recruits to think outside of the box to solve the complex scenarios SEAL teams are faced with.

While the recruits were not allowed rest they did eat four meals a day. Food was the only comfort during hell week. Each recruit consumed approximately five to seven thousand calories a day and still lost weight. Daily medical inspections were conducted, as the worn down men were susceptible to illness and infection.

The constant log PT and the swim a mile, followed by run a mile evolutions were taking their toll. By Friday there were only 30 recruits left. Over half of class 86 had been dropped for performance or rang out.

Blue went to the famous mud flats where SEAL recruits trained. The mud flats were referred to as Camp Swampy. The expanse of mud was unforgiving and the instructors made sure the recruits got plenty of slimy bottom samples. Blue was chest deep in mud and freezing. This was by far the coldest that he had ever been and he was shivering uncontrollably. An instructor paced back and forth in front of the men. He was drinking a piping hot cup of coffee. The instructor said calmly "would any of you like some coffee"? There was a pregnant *pause before he continued and said " boys you can have all the coffee you want if you just ring the bell and quit".*

*Blue was suffering; the stress of the week and the cold mud played with his head. In a moment of weakness Blue decided to quit. With less than 24 hours left in hell week Blue had enough. He told his squad that he was going to ring out because he was to cold to go on. The caked on mud hid the tears rolling down Blue's face. His squad members rallied around shouting words of encouragement and support. The minutes seemed like hours as Blue searched the depths of his soul to find a hidden reserve. Blue shrugged off the pain and gritted his teeth before saying that he was ok and going to make it.*

*That night around 2:00 AM the instructors directed the recruits to pitch their tents and prepare to get a couple hours of rest. The recruits were surprised and elated at the news. Two men to a tent, the trainees quickly set up. The muddy, wet and cold men crawled inside the tents for some much needed sleep.*

*A few moments later the instructor's next directive rolled forth across the land. He advised the recruits that they would have to rotate standing watch. Each man would pull a shift that was two minutes long. The recruit on duty was instructed to March back and forth in front of the row of tents. Every 30 seconds he had to yell out the time and say "all is well at beautiful camp swampy down by the sea". Instead of getting a couple hours of rest the recruits were kept up by the constant yelling and the rotations of the two-minute watches.*

*With camp swampy complete it was back into the IBS for more ocean paddling. The early morning fog made it difficult for the men to see as the instructors pushed the exhausted recruits toward the next evolution. Saturday morning after eating the class mustered outside of the chow hall. A SEAL instructor casually said, " Class 86 secure from hell week, you people made it". Blue and his class completed the hell week evolutions with just three hours of total sleep for the week. The recruits struggled back to the barracks where Blue collapsed in his bunk and slept for 22 hours straight. Blue's journal continues:*

2-9 Nov 75

Well, it's been hell. We finished hell week yesterday morning. It was really Hell!! We got about 3 hours of sleep the whole week. And, we were always wet and in those fucking IBS's. We must have paddled a hundred miles. I hated every moment of hell week. I wanted to quit every day. But, I hung in there. I was one of two blacks to make it through hell week in three years. I slept from 11 AM on Saturday till 9 AM on Sunday morning. I was really tired. My body is so sore. I shall never forget hell week. I thank God that I made it. I still really haven't decided if this is really what I want to do.

9-15 Nov 75

Today was my birthday and I'm twenty years old. I had to muster this morning at 4AM to turn in another PLO (Patrol Leader's Order) so I wasn't too happy about that. I've been deliberating whether I should go home for Christmas. I want to go but it's go to cost a lot of money. I wanted to buy a new car. Last week was a pretty tough week. We had night classes every night. And, PT got harder. We learned to work with the compass and map. We went to the mountains Thursday all day for a compass course. We had a 4 mile timed run on Friday and I did a 27:28 and the O'course in 12:19 my best time. We had a party Friday night. I also had Duty. I drank before duty. There was a lot of booze left over from the party so I got it all. A few of the guys took me out to dinner for pizza tonight for my birthday. No one back home sent me anything for my birthday.

16-19 Nov 75

For the past three days we have been going to the rifle range to learn to shoot the M16 and pistol. Today we had qualifications for expert. I didn't do to well with the M16 but I got expert with the pistol. I was surprised that I did so well with the pistol. I've decided to go home for Christmas. It's going to cost me a lot of money but I'm going home anyway. Today I met a guy in BUD/S who's from Fort Pierce Central High school. I used to swim against him. I can't believe it a guy right next door from me. He knows some of my buddies from high school. Only five more days of First Phase and it will all be over.

A new instructor will be with us in Second Phase. I'm asking God to help me along the way.

20 Nov.

Today we had lifesaving at the pool. It was all right but the water was cold. We had a pretty tough run this morning in the soft sand. I heard one of our instructors was telling people all up and down the coast about me and the other black guy in my class. That makes me feel kind of proud. Tonight we had knot tying in the 50-foot water tower.

Before we started one of my boat crew asked the instructor what would happen if we passed out on the way down. The instructor barked "don't worry about that because I will revive your dumb ass before I make you attempt the evolution again. So we will cross that bridge when we get to it trainee, any one else have a stupid question?" After that comment we all waited in silence to plunge into the deep water when commanded. We started out by holding our breath and going down to tie knots at shallow depths. We increased the depth gradually going deeper and deeper. At the end we had to hold our breath and swim down 50 feet to the bottom of the tower and meet an instructor who was waiting in a bubble that had compressed air being piped down. At first I was terrified. I went to the bottom with our Senior Chief. After I made it to the bottom, I realized it was really easy. I think that I was just psyching myself out. The next challenge was to ascend to the top while exhaling all of the compressed air out of your lungs. The worst part of the assent was that an instructor would accompany you kicking you in the chest, to insure that you released all of the compressed air from your lungs. Keeping compressed air in your lungs can cause divers to get the bends and die. This whole training is basically mental. I received a birthday card from mother today. That makes me feel very happy. It's nice to know that someone is thinking about you.

21-26 Nov 75

Today was our last day of First Phase. No more of getting up at 4 o'clock in the morning. I did my best time in the 4-mile timed run today (26:18). I did my best in the o'course with a 12:15. I'm the slowest in the class in the o'course. I'm really glad we are leaving first phase. But, I'm sure Second Phase is a lot harder. I received a letter from home today. Seems everything is ok. Tonight I just set back and relaxed. I drank some wine with my teammates to celebrate. I passed my Phase Test with 79%. I thank God I made it through First Phase.

27 Nov 75

Today was Thanksgiving and I had a great dinner and time over at my buddies' girlfriends house. About five of us guys went over there. I called mother today. She says everything is ok. My sister says the football team lost every game this year. The basketball team is starting off on a good foot. I thank God for giving me life up to this day. I pray that I get to see many more.

28 Nov.

Today was our first day of second phase and I think it's going to be hell. We spray painted our helmets from green to red to show we were in phase two. The instructor can run like a wild horse. We are going to learn a lot of stuff. I am having a little problem learning the stuff that they are teaching us. We had classes on nautical charts, beach terminology and surf reports. Today was payday and we got paid our demolition pay for a month ($55). I'm still not sure if I'll be going home for Christmas.

I just might stay right here and buy me a car. They told us that our trip to San Clemente Island is going to be a motherfucker. It's right after we get back from Christmas Leave.

1 Dec.
I fell back on the run today. I really did shitty. The instructor was running like crazy. I did terrible. We are learning how to make maps and I am not getting this shit they are teaching us.

3 Dec 75
I fell back on another run today after PT. I don't know why I wouldn't stay up. I'm having a bad pain in my hipbone; I hope it isn't anything serious. I guess those instructors think that I am a sorry turkey. This second phase is so demanding. We are going to be in the water a lot starting tomorrow. We've been having homework every night and I'm not getting this material good enough. I'm asking God to help me along the way. A Brother from SEAL Team One was killed last night on a jump. I would hate to go all the way through this training then go jump out of plane and get killed.
Heavenly Father, please help me get the material they are giving out.

7 Dec 75
I've been studying for the tests on Wednesday.
If I can just past these tests, I'll be able to go home at Christmas. Tomorrow we start Water Week. The majority of the week will be

in the water. I ran in a 3-mile race in San Diego this morning. I won a tee shirt for getting a time under 20 minutes.

8-14 Dec 75

Last week was water week and we did a lot of Hydrographic Reconnaissance in the ocean, San Diego Bay and in Mission Bay. We also did reconnaissance at night. The water was always cold. I made an 82 on one test and 76 on another. Friday night an instructor kicked me and four other guys out of Danny's bar. We will get punished for it tomorrow. I've been going out at the club here; I never danced this much in my life. I think that I'm going to do the same at home. So far the instructors haven't been fucking with me in Second Phase. But, they get the other brother in my class wet every day.

If everything goes ok, I shall be going home on Friday for Christmas. I haven't told anyone at home yet. Tomorrow is payday and I really need the money to get my tickets. We start learning Demolition tomorrow. It's going to be tough. I am going to give it my best. I'm asking God to help me through.

16 Dec 75

Today really wasn't my day. I got wet during the Obstacle course. Then we went to the water and I got caught wearing a cheater. A cheater is a thin wet suit that can only be worn if authorized by the instructor staff. There were about 15 of us. We all got written up and tomorrow we will get a goon squad circus.

He fucked us up at the bay too. He made us take off all of our rubber and we had to do all kinds of races. We had to do sugar cookies. A sugar cookie is when you get wet and then roll around until you are covered in beach sand.

Throughout the evolution the instructor would stick us in the surf and insist we sing him a song. I must have sung "Anchors Away" a dozen times.

I made an 80 on my test today. Tomorrow we have a TNT test. My instructor actually makes sure that I take salt tablets every day to help with cramps. I think that he's really concerned. So I have to put out to let him know that I appreciate it. So far I don't have a way back to San Diego. But I'm still going home.

*Blue went back home for his two weeks of vacation. Its 1976 now and Blue rang in the New Year with friends and family in Stuart Florida. When he returned to BUD/S training his class went to San Clemente Island for a week. It was just like hell week in a way. They got up early in the morning and did PT. San Clemente Island is a sparse camp with tin buildings. The terrain was rocky and full of hills. Before the trainees could enter the mess hall to eat they had to perform a series of pull-ups and bar dips. The trainees were given unlimited ammunition to practice with. They were able to select from a wide variety of firearms as well. Instructors wanted the recruits to become expertly familiar with these tools of the trade.*

*There were two long distance ocean swims. Blue did not complete the first three and one half mile swim. The water was cold and his body cramped up.*

*Blue did complete his five and one half mile swimming evolution.*

*Blue can't remember how he made it back to the barracks after the swim. He somehow survived the grueling physical test.*

*They conducted a lot of explosives training on the island and Blue passed his final demolition test. One of the recruit officers did not pass the final demo test and was dropped from BUD/S by the SEAL instructors. Blues journal entries are less frequent as the demanding classroom work consumes the days.*

19 Jan 76

Today was just basic stuff. A few guys form SEAL Team One are in our class. They will be with us till the end of the Phase. I called home yesterday; I only talked to my sister. She said that mother has lost her job. So I'll have to help her out a little. I won $15 on the Dallas Pittsburgh game yesterday, Super Bowl X. I wrote an old girlfriend tonight and told her how I felt about her. God I hope it does some good.

20 Jan.

Today was a pretty easy day. I got my best time on the obstacle course 11:13. We spent the rest of the day in the classroom getting lectures on SEAL Ambush techniques, Assault Tactics and Insertion/Extraction methods. The classroom time is kind of boring.

22 Jan.

Today we had a 4 mile timed run. Everyone was slow. We ran down to the North Island. I got a 29:36 on the run. We did insertion and extraction by boat today. It was kind of cool playing a real SEAL. We also did patrolling out on the beach tonight. We fill out our dream sheets tomorrow. I am picking SEAL Team 2 or UDT 21 because those are the only east coast teams. Class 85 will be graduating tomorrow. My class is now the senior training class at the compound. We have 9 more weeks to go!

26 Jan.

The weekend was all right; last night I watched the break out for hell week for class 87. It was very funny; I guess the guys in class 85 thought the same thing about us. Today during PT we did 500 four count back flutter kicks. I can't believe we did that many. I was so tired I was not able to stay up on the run. I got written up for falling behind. I think that that is about my sixth write up in Second Phase. MY shit is so weak. But for the past few days, my stomach has been fucked up and my legs just don't feel like they use to in the First Phase. They never use to give me trouble. I think the biggest thing is that I don't eat breakfast. My morale is really going down. I'm getting to the point that I really don't like any of the instructors. They are always fucking with me. I think that these next nine weeks are going to be pretty tough. I have watch tonight and I had it yesterday too. Heavenly Father, please help me get myself together.

27 Jan 76

Today we did repelling, and it was scary at first. I mean that I was really scared. We did it from the tower at 50 feet. You stand on the edge of the tower with only a rope around your waist. The hardest part was the first jump. You jump and free fall, you hold the rope out in your hand away from the body. In order to stop or brake, you bring your hand in to your side. What a new experience. On Friday we get to do the real thing from a helicopter.

We also did our last O'Course in Second Phase. I have to do well in our last 4 mile run tomorrow.

*February 3rd through February 13th the class returned to San Clemente Island. Here they honed their skills in land warfare. The evolutions ran late into the night, as the trainees grew competent using their weapons.*

*The island training culminated with all the trainee squads having to complete a lengthy mission. The last night on the island the recruits had a chance to unwind.*

16 Feb 76

We got back from San Clemente Island Friday night. The trip was all right, but wet. We were up all night cleaning weapons. I got to shoot all kinds of weapons. We did a lot of patrolling. The last night we were there we had a party. The instructors got a lot friendlier with us. So now we are out of Second Phase. Third Phase starts tomorrow. We've got seven more weeks of this bullshit. I can't wait till it's over. I'm going to have to study really hard for the tests. I think that the instructors think that I am going to have problems. My Mother is working again and I'm back to saving money.

*Tuesday February 17, 1976 the third and final phase began. The trainees spray-painted their helmets blue to signify that they were in the scuba diving phase of BUD/S.*

*With seven weeks to go the evolutions focused on underwater operations. Along with mastering dive techniques Blue had to become proficient in Anatomy and Physiology, Diving Medical Diseases Associated with the Primary and Secondary Effects of Pressure, Air Diving Tables and Mixed Gas Diving Tables. The next few weeks of training kept Blue's head spinning. The lectures and diving tests were difficult. Every evolution had to be successfully negotiated for Theo to continue.*

*When diving Blue remembers how beautiful the long flowing strands of kelp were that grew up from the ocean floor. The kelp strands were more than one hundred feet long and swimming among them was a surreal experience. Blue's vision of the kelp changed dramatically when the instructor directed the trainees to take a mouthful of the putrid water plant and swallow. Blue writes:*

01 Mar 76

Today we had a 120-foot bounce dive in the ocean. It was very cold down there. Diving has been kind of strange, just being able to breathe under water is really neat. I like it but I really hate the cold water. We have only five more weeks to go. I have to take a make-up test tomorrow on Dive Tables. I have to pass it.

07 Mar 76

I passed my test Friday and now I'm a certified Scuba Diver. We start the Mark IV Dive system tomorrow and it will last for two weeks. The Mark IV system is semi-closed and uses a mixture of nitrogen and oxygen. The system allows you to conduct deep dives. I hear it could be dangerous. With four more weeks to go, I'm praying to god to help me make it through.


14 Mar 76

The weekend was all right. I went out dancing with a few chicks over at the Miramar Air Base. Friday night, a few of us guys in the class went to the Naval Training Center and on 32$^{nd}$ Street to the club. I was very down during some moments of the weekend. I think that I'm getting home sick. The closer we get to graduation, the more I think of home. I'm sort of worried about the two tests we are go to have next week. Diving tables are pretty tough. I've got to pass the test!! That's the only thing that I'm worried about. I received a letter from my old girlfriend last week and man did that brighten up my day. I was so happy to hear from her. I still think that I'm in love with her.

She says she's going to take me out the next time I'm home. Another girl wrote me a letter too. She says she's in love with me. I had a little incident with her one night when I was home for Christmas. I had sex with her and afterwards, she began to tell me how much she loved me and how she felt about me. I tried to explain to her that I was not interested.

When I told her that, she began to cry. Man, I kind of felt bad. I think that she's just young and doesn't know what she is saying. We have only three weeks to go now and we are all done. My Orders came in and I am assigned to UDT-21. I am so close now, and feeling high speed low drag. I'm asking God to help me make it through the next three weeks.

15 Mar 76

We had two dives today and one was tonight and it was fucked. We got off to a late start and I didn't hit on target and I got my shit jumped into by the instructor. I think that I'm giving him a very bad impression of me. I'm very concerned about that. I received my income tax refund check today, $130 and I also got paid today too. I just can't wait till this training is over. I miss my family. We have a big test tomorrow, I'd like to ace it, and I'll try.

18 Mar.

Last night we had a dive and it was sneak attack training. It was sort of scary being under a ship and placing a mine underneath it.

21 Mar.

We had a 120-foot bounce dive yesterday in the ocean. I got seasick again. So they would not let me use the Mark VI rig. My swim buddy and I had to use open circuit. While we were at the bottom, a teammate was swimming in front of me. He accidentally kicked my mouthpiece out of my mouth. I almost shit in my pants. I thought I was a goner.

But, I just kept my cool and reached around and grabbed my mouthpiece and put it back into my mouth. Today I went and spent the day on the beach with some chicks. The girls were pretty friendly but just friends.

I also went dancing with them the other night. We have two more weeks of training to go. I'm asking God to be with me.

28 Mar 76

Only one more week to go now and only two more dives to do, one tomorrow morning and one tomorrow night. We will have a pretty tough PT, I'm sure. I hate those eight count body builders. If I keep my stuff together, and pass that test Tuesday, I got it made. I'm asking God to help me through this last week. I think that when I leave, I'm going to miss my classmates. Last night I went to San Diego State to dance. The chicks were really weird. I wish that someone from home could come to my graduation.

01 Apr 76

I only have a few more hours before graduation now, I guess I'm happy, but I'm not as excited as I was at coming here.
I called home and they said that they wouldn't be able to pick me up at the airport on Saturday. I got a feeling that I'm not going to have a good time at home. Heavenly father, I'm almost there and I thank you very much.

02 Apr 76

Today I graduated from BUD/S and I'm very proud of myself. There were 17 of us that made it plus three Corpsmen. I went out to dinner with one of my classmates. I was sort of bummed out after the graduation because none of the people that I invited came. I said good-bye to all the instructors and everyone. My girls kissed me good-bye; I'm going to miss this old place. I thank God for making it possible for me to make it through

*Blue's graduation from BUD/S was one the most significant accomplishments of his life. Blue started with seventy other trainees in class 86. The seventeen that finished put the class success rate at 11.9%. Consider the fact that six blacks started the class and Theo was one of two to finish. His chances of successfully completing the course drop to 4.2%. Blue went on to successfully complete Army Jump School before beginning his tour of duty in UDT 21 as a United States Navy SEAL.*

*Theo was discharged from the Navy two-year's later and attended college where he met his wife. Blue graduated from Florida State University. He then spent 10 years in The United Stated Army as an Intelligence Officer. Theo has two daughters and has been a Police Officer for many years. Blue enjoys motivating others to be the best that they can be.*

*It has been a long road for Theodis "Blue" Springer and every time he faces adversity he flashes back to BUD/S training where the "Only Easy Day Was Yesterday".*

# Gallery

Blue is a sophomore posing with his High School swim team.
Circa 1970

Actual Cover shot of BUD/S Training Manual circa 1975

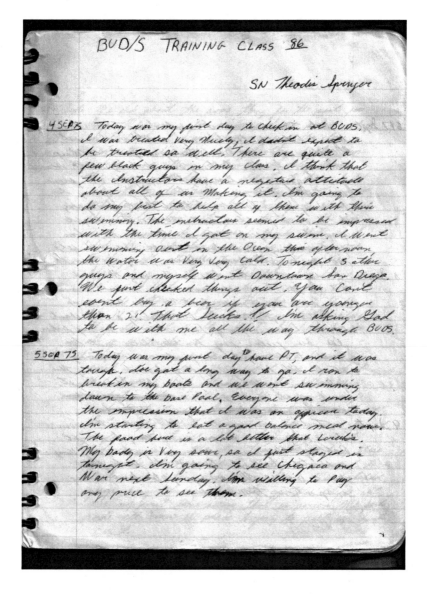

Blue's First Journal Entry on Day 1 of BUD/S
September 4, 1975

63

Blue during first phase on the Silver Strand (Night Training).

BUD/S class 86 at San Clemente Island (Demolition Phase).
Blue is second from the right.

BUD/S
Demolition Training
San Clemente Island

65

BUD/S obstacle named "WEAVER" The trainees had to weave their way through on their stomachs.

The 50-foot Dive Tower at Coronado Springs

This is the BUD/S obstacle "DIRTY NAME". Recruits had to leap from one log to the next moving up and over the obstacle.

In the background is the infamous BUD/S obstacle "SLIDE FOR LIFE".

All Photos on this page are circa 1975/76

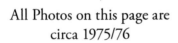

SPECIAL OPERATIONS DEPARTMENT
NAVAL AMPHIBIOUS SCHOOL CORONADO
SAN DIEGO, CALIFORNIA 92155
BASIC UNDERWATER DEMOLITION/SEAL TRAINING DEPARTMENT

5313-S-(1)-13-A

## IBS COMMANDS

**LAND:**

a. "STAND BY YOUR BOAT"
Coxwain at stern. 6 paddlers standing by port and starboard 1, 2, and 3 positions facing forward (aft if situation calls for it)

b. "PREPARE FOR LOW CARRY"
(or Shoulder Carry or Head Carry)
Crew bends over and grasps carrying handles

c. "UP BOAT"
Low Carry - Stand up to a crouched position with arms extended and boat handling at about knee level

SHOULDER CARRY OR HEAD CARRY
Raise to shoulder or head level

d. "PREPARE FOR DOWN BOAT"
Make preparations for lowering boat

e. "DOWN BOAT"
Lower boat gently to the ground

f. "FORWARD MARCH"
Portage carry

g. "DOUBLE TIME, MARCH"
Portage carry

h. "HIT THE SURF"
Execute with boat at Low Carry

i. "CREW HALT"
All hands halt in place

**SURF AND UNDERWAY**

a. "ONE'S IN"
PORT AND STARBOARD - One climb in and commence paddlin

b. "TWO'S IN" - "THREE'S IN"
Both two's (and three's) climb aboard and take up the rythm of the stroke paddler (#1 starboard)

c. "GIVE WAY TOGETHER"
All paddlers dip and pull together

d. "WAY ENOUGH"
All paddlers rest paddles across their knees, blades outboard and in a horizontal position

e. "HOLD WATER" (HOLD WATER PORT OR HOLD WATER STARBOARD)
Those ordered to hold, dip their full blade in a vertical position and held it that way until oredred otherwise. (Others, if all are not ordered to hold, continue paddling)

f. "BACK WATER" (BACK WATER PORT OR BACK WATER STARBOARD)
Paddle in a reverse motion AS ORDERED AND CONTINUE UNTIL OREDRED OTHERWISE

This is an actual page from the IBS training Manual issued to Blue.
IBS = Inflatable Boat Small. An IBS was the primary SEAL
deployment watercraft.
Circa 1975

Blue's Navy SEAL gear
Circa 1975

After a grueling 5-½-mile ocean swim, Blue can't remember
this photo being taken due to extreme fatigue.

Blue relaxes in UDT shirt, shorts and boots.
This was the standard BUD/S training attire.

Blue during land warfare training
San Clemente Island California.
Circa 1976

# BASIC UNDERWATER DEMOLITION/SEAL

## TRAINING COURSE

# GRADUATION EXERCISES
# CLASS 86

### NAVAL AMPHIBIOUS SCHOOL
### CORONADO, CALIFORNIA

**1330 FRIDAY**      **2 APRIL 1976**

Theodis "Blue" Springer
United States Navy SEAL

United States Navy SEAL Code – Est 2005

In times of war or uncertainty there is a special breed of warrior ready to answer our Nation's call. A common man with uncommon desire to succeed.

Forged by adversity, he stands alongside America's finest special operations forces to serve his country, the American people, and protect their way of life.

I am that man.

My Trident is a symbol of honor and heritage. Bestowed upon me by the heroes that have gone before, it embodies the trust of those I have sworn to protect. By wearing the Trident I accept the responsibility of my chosen profession and way of life. It is a privilege that I must earn every day.

My loyalty to Country and Team is beyond reproach. I humbly serve as a guardian to my fellow Americans always ready to defend those who are unable to defend themselves. I do not advertise the nature of my work, nor seek recognition for my actions. I voluntarily accept the inherent hazards of my profession, placing the welfare and security of others before my own.

I serve with honor on and off the battlefield. The ability to control my emotions and my actions, regardless of circumstance, sets me apart from other men.

Uncompromising integrity is my standard. My character and honor are steadfast. My word is my bond.

We expect to lead and be led. In the absence of orders I will take charge, lead my teammates and accomplish the mission. I lead by example in all situations.

I will never quit. I persevere and thrive on adversity. My Nation expects me to be physically harder and mentally stronger than my enemies. If knocked down, I will get back up, every time. I will draw on every remaining ounce of strength to protect my teammates and to accomplish our mission. I am never out of the fight.

We demand discipline. We expect innovation. The lives of my teammates and the success of our mission depend on me - my technical skill, tactical proficiency, and attention to detail. My training is never complete.

We train for war and fight to win. I stand ready to bring the full spectrum of combat power to bear in order to achieve my mission and the goals established by my country. The execution of my duties will be swift and violent when required yet guided by the very principles that I serve to defend.

Brave men have fought and died building the proud tradition and feared reputation that I am bound to uphold. In the worst of conditions, the legacy of my teammates steadies my resolve and silently guides my every deed.

I will not fail.

CPSIA information can be obtained at www.ICGtesting.com
Printed in the USA
BVOW03s1838150414

350738BV00001B/77/P